THE SECRET LIFE OF DOGS
CARTOONS BY DAVID SIPRESS

A PLUME BOOK

PLUME
Published by the Penguin Group
Penguin Books USA Inc., 375 Hudson Street, New York, New York 10014, U.S.A.
Penguin Books Ltd, 27 Wrights Lane, London W8 5TZ, England
Penguin Books Australia Ltd, Ringwood, Victoria, Australia
Penguin Books Canada Ltd, 2801 John Street, Markham, Ontario, Canada L3R 1B4
Penguin Books (N.Z.) Ltd, 182–190 Wairau Road, Auckland 10, New Zealand
Penguin Books Ltd, Registered Offices: Harmondsworth, Middlesex, England

First published by Plume, an imprint of New American Library, a division of Penguin
Books USA Inc.

First Printing, September, 1990
10 9 8 7 6 5 4 3 2 1

 REGISTERED TRADEMARK—MARCA REGISTRADA

Library of Congress Cataloging-in-Publication Data

Sipress, David.
    The secret life of dogs : cartoons / by David Sipress.
        p.   cm.
    ISBN 0-452-26494-4
    1. Dogs—Caricatures and cartoons.   2. American wit and humor,
Pictorial.   I. Title.
NC1429.S532A4   1990
741.5'973—dc20   90-34425
                                                           CIP

Printed in the United States of America

BOOKS ARE AVAILABLE AT QUANTITY DISCOUNTS WHEN USED TO PROMOTE PRODUCTS OR SERVICES.
FOR INFORMATION PLEASE WRITE TO PREMIUM MARKETING DIVISION, PENGUIN BOOKS USA INC.,
375 HUDSON STREET, NEW YORK, NEW YORK 10014.

Go on, Sparky... Network!

It's that animal magnetism...

SIPRESS

①

②

③

④

SIPRESS

SIPRESS

THE GREAT DEBATE:

① DOGS ARE INCREDIBLY STUPID.

OH YEAH? WELL CATS ARE THE WORLD'S BIGGEST SNOBS!

② DOGS NOT ONLY ARE STUPID, THEY'RE ALSO DIRTY, SMELLY, AND CLUMSY.

HEY! WELL, WE'RE SMART ENOUGH TO BE NICE! YOU CATS ARE ALL COLD, SELFISH, EGOMANIACS!!

③ WE CATS HAVE PRIDE IN OURSELVES, SELF-ESTEEM. DOGS FALL IN LOVE WITH ANY JERK THAT FEEDS THEM. MY POINT AGAIN: DOGS ARE DUMB!

OH YEAH, SMARTY PANTS? WELL, I'LL HAVE YOU KNOW THAT DOGS ARE MAN'S BEST FRIEND!!

④

I REST MY CASE.

SIPRESS

DOGGIE HEALTH TIPS

Give him regular exercise.

Help him avoid stress.

DOGGIE HEALTH TIPS

Limit his diet.

Floss after every meal.

SiPRESS

And just remember: Daddy got you out of that
nasty pet store because he hopes you'll act really
cute and friendly in the park, especially around
attractive, single women.

You said not to "beg," and I completely agree, that begging is demeaning, unseemly, behavior, so I want to say, and this comes from a really powerful place inside of me, that I feel I truly deserve a piece of that lamb chop.

SIPRESS

SIPRESS

We can get the pug, honey, but I really think the poodle looks better with that coat.

PREVIOUSLY UNKNOWN BREEDS

Carlo, we need to have a little chat about your breath.

Dogs used to be our thing, but now we're into kids.

③

④

SIPRESS

SIPRESS

①

②

③

④

SIPRESS

NEW TRICKS!!

Teach Your Dog To...

Sipress

SIPRESS

SIPRESS

Oh, yeah? Well, if I'm so afraid of intimacy, how do you explain _this_??

WHAT THE DOG HEARD

SIPRESS

SIPRESS

DOGS WHO
LOVE MEN
WHO LOVE
WOMEN WHO
HATE DOGS.

by hand

SIPRESS

SIPRESS

But enough about me! How was your day?

SIPRESS

I thought "house train" meant you train him to go in the house.

SIPRESS

They might have mentioned that the damned thing was shedding!

SIPRESS

The Adventures of... **NEUROTIC DOG**

SIPRESS

Well, we were on our way to the store, but then we got into this _really_ interesting discussion about Hegel.

Sorry, Waldo.

COUNTRY DOG vs. N.Y. CITY DOG

I dont need <u>them</u> to take me out every time I have to go.

Oh yeah? Well, every time I <u>do</u> go, <u>they</u> have to bend down and pick it up for me!

SIPRESS

I said "heel," he thought I meant "heal," and the rest is history.

O.K.! O.K.! We'll go for a walk!!

SIPRESS

NEW TRICKS!!
Teach Your Dog To ...

MAKE DECISIONS

BEG FORGIVENESS

Excuse me, would you tell the guy in the plaid
jacket that his dog is getting very impatient?

SIPRESS

You know, just once, I'd like you to take
<u>me</u> for a walk!

SIPRESS

SIPRESS